MW00882086

Dog Sweaters Crocheting

Sweaters will Make Your Dog Smile with Delight

Copyright © 2020

All rights reserved.

DEDICATION

The author and publisher have provided this e-book to you for your personal use only. You may not make this e-book publicly available in any way. Copyright infringement is against the law. If you believe the copy of this e-book you are reading infringes on the author's copyright, please notify the publisher at: https://us.macmillan.com/piracy

Contents

Easy Crochet Dog Sweater

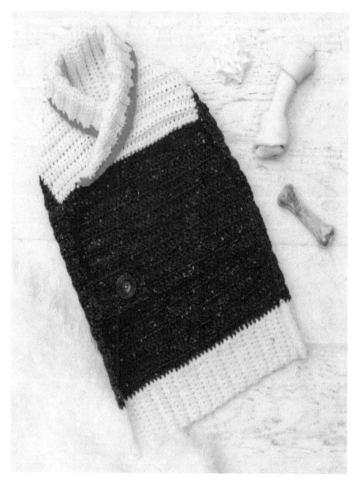

It is very easy to find cute free crochet dog sweater patterns for small dogs. However, if you have a larger dog, then it's not quite so simple. Many designers haven't adapted their designs to fit bigger dogs. That's not a problem with this great pattern. The designer offers nine sizes, suitable to fit any size of dog that you might have. And what a stylish, elegant design!

Materials:

- Choosing a yarn for a crochet dog sweater pattern feels a little like designing for a baby. The yarn needs to be soft AND practical. And the ability to machine wash is essential.

- Tapestry needle

- Size K (6.5 mm) crochet hook

- Stitch markers or safety pins

- (2-4) 1.5" wooden buttons

Abbreviations and Glossary (US Terms):

ch – chain

dc – double crochet

dc2tog – double crochet two together

hdc – half double crochet

hdcblo – half double crochet through the back loop only

PM – place marker

RS – right side

sc – single crochet

sk – skip

st(s) – stitch(es)

WS – wrong side

yo – yarn over

Sizes:

XXXS, XXS, XS, S, M, L1, L2, 1X, 2X

Choose your size based primarily on the dog's length from the base of the tail to the dog's collar and secondarily on the dog's chest circumference at its widest part. L1 and L2 difference is based on the length of of dog's back.

Gauge:

Main Sweater: 13 dc x 7.5 rows= 4"

Ribbing: 13 hdc x 8 rows through the back loop only = 4"

BOTTOM RIBBING

Notes:

• Ribbing is worked sideways.

• Ch 2 at beginning of row does not count as a stitch.

• Row 2 and beyond are worked through the back loop only of the hdc stitches (hdcblo).

Using Color A:

Foundation Row: Ch 6 (8, 9, 11, 12, 13, 14, 16, 17).

Row 1: Sk 2 ch, hdc in each ch; turn. [4 (6, 7, 9, 10, 11, 12, 14, 15)]

Row 2: Ch 2, hdcblo in each hdc; turn. [4 (6, 7, 9, 10, 11, 12, 14, 15)]

Rows 3-16 (22, 25, 28, 31, 34, 34, 37, 44): Ch 2, hdcblo in each hdc; turn. [4 (6, 7, 9, 10, 11, 12, 14, 15)]

Do not fasten off. Rotate ribbing 90 degrees. Row 1 of Back piece will be worked into long edge of ribbing.

BACK

Notes:

• Row 1 is worked at a frequency of approx. 3 sc per 1 visual ribbing ridge (which is 2 hdc rows).

• Ch 3 at beginning of row counts as first dc.

Using Color A still attached:

Row 1 (RS): Ch 1, sc 26 (36, 40, 46, 51, 55, 55, 60, 72) along long edge, completing final yo of last sc with Color B; turn. [26 (36, 40, 46, 51, 55, 55, 60, 72)]

Using Color B:

Row 2 (WS): Ch 3, sk first st, dc in each sc; turn. [26 (36, 40, 46, 51, 55, 55, 60, 72)]

Rows 3-12 (17, 21, 25, 28, 32, 36, 41, 44): Ch 3, sk first st, dc in each dc; turn. [26 (36, 40, 46, 51, 55, 55, 60, 72)]

Note:

Decreases should begin when sweater length reaches from end of dog's back (where tail is) to approximately the front of dog's front legs. If you're finding the sweater piece too long, simply remove a couple of rows from the back section and move on to decreasing. Similarly, for a long, thin dog, feel free to add additional rows of double crochet before decreasing.

Decreasing:

Row 1 (WS): Ch 3, sk first st, dc2tog, dc in each dc until 2 remain, dc2tog; turn. [24 (34, 38, 44, 49, 53, 53, 58, 70)]

Rows 2-3 (4, 5, 6, 7, 8, 9, 10, 11): Ch 3, sk first st, dc2tog, dc in each dc until 2 remain, dc2tog; turn. 2 sts decreased each row

At end of Row 8, there should be 20 (28, 30, 34, 37, 39, 37, 40, 50) dc. Fasten off leaving 25" tail.

BELLY

Notes:

• Ch 3 at beginning of row counts as first dc.

Using Color B:

Foundation Row: Ch 20 (27, 30, 34, 37, 40, 40, 43, 52).

Row 1 (RS): Sk 3 ch, dc in each ch; turn. [18 (25, 28, 32, 35, 38, 38, 41, 50)]

Row 2 (WS): Ch 3, sk first st, dc in each dc; turn. [18 (25, 28, 32, 35, 38, 38, 41, 50)]

Rows 3-7 (10, 12, 14, 16, 18, 20, 23, 24): Ch 3, sk first st, dc in each dc; turn. [18 (25, 28, 32, 35, 38, 38, 41, 50)]

Note:

If you added or eliminated rows of double crochet before decreasing in the Back, considering doing the same thing with the Belly.

COLLAR RIBBING

Notes:

• Ribbing is worked sideways.

• Ch 2 at beginning of row does not count as a stitch.

• Row 2 and beyond are worked through the back loop only of the hdc stitches (hdcblo).

Foundation Row: Ch 16 (21, 23, 26, 28, 31, 31, 33, 39).

Row 1 (WS): Sk 2 ch, hdc in each ch; turn. [14 (19, 21, 24, 26, 29, 29, 31, 37)]

Row 2 (RS): \Ch 2, hdcblo in each hdc; turn. [14 (19, 21, 24, 26, 29, 29, 31, 37)]

Rows 3-18 (26, 29, 34, 37, 40, 41, 46, 53): Ch 2, hdcblo in each hdc; turn. [14 (19, 21, 24, 26, 29, 29, 31, 37)]

Fasten off.

SIDE FASTENERS

Notes:

• Side fasteners are optional. See "Overall Pattern + Sizing Notes" for more details.

• Ch 3 at beginning of row counts as first dc.

• For the 1X and 2X sizes, you may choose to add an additional button hole to each fastener to make it extra secure. To do this, work the Center Row (buttonhole) after you've completed Row 2 three times. Then work 3 more rows of regular double crochet before completing one more Center Row (buttonhole). Finish with 3 rows of double crochet and the last row

Make 2 using Color B:

Foundation Row: Ch 8 (8, 11, 11, 11, 11, 11, 16, 16).

Row 1: Sk first ch, sc in each ch; turn. [7, (7, 10, 10, 10, 10, 10, 15, 15)]

Row 2: Ch 3, sk first st, dc in each sc; turn. [7, (7, 10, 10, 10, 10, 10, 15, 15)]

Repeat Row 2 another 0 (0, 1, 1, 2, 2, 3, 3, 4) times

Center Row (buttonhole): Ch 3, sk first st, dc in next 2 dc, ch 1, sk 1 dc, dc in each dc; turn. [6, (6, 9, 9, 9, 9, 9, 14, 14) and 1 ch-1]

Next Row: Ch 3, sk first st, dc in each dc and ch-1; turn. [7, (7, 10, 10, 10, 10, 10, 15, 15)]

Repeat Row 2 another 0 (0, 1, 1, 2, 2, 3, 3, 4) times

Last Row: Ch 1, sc in each dc. [7, (7, 10, 10, 10, 10, 10, 15, 15)]

Fasten off leaving 20" tail.

Fastener will have 5 (5, 7, 7, 9, 9, 11, 11, 13) rows.

FINISHING

1. Attaching Back to Belly: With RS of Back and belly piece facing, align last (top) row of Belly with Row 12 (17, 21, 25, 28, 32, 36, 41, 44) of Back (last row before decreasing). Pin if desired.

2. Attaching Collar: Turn sweater RS out. Align last row of Collar with top edge of Belly as pictured in photo C. Pin if desired. Using Color B, seam last row of Collar to top edge of Belly beginning at left edge of Collar.

Continuing with yarn attached, seam row edges of Collar to Back working across decrease section, continuing across straight edge, then across next decrease section. Finish by seaming first row of Collar to last row of Belly behind section that is already seamed and beginning with left edges of Belly and Collar aligned.

3. Collar Trim: Using Color C, attach yarn at bottom front corner of Collar.

With inside of Collar facing you:

Row 1: Ch 1, sc evenly around Collar edge, ending where Collar meets Belly inside sweater; turn.

Row 2: Ch 1, sc in each sc, ending where Row 1 began.

Fasten off and weave in remaining ends.

Pink Dog Sweater

This is another free crochet dog sweater recipe. It has step-by-step instructions for measuring your dog. Moreover, it shows nine different common dog sizes, including three that have wider chests that normal. Each size includes a list of dogs that size usually fits.

Nevertheless, the recipe gives you instructions for working the pattern to suit the measurements you take. You can actually work the pattern in any crochet stitch that you like, so you have a lot of freedom to get creative with this design.

1. Cast on your yarn and make a chain the length of the Back (B) measurement. Be sure your back ends at a good point for both the tummy and back - as in, you don't want your dog weeing on the sweater, so don't make it too long ;)

2. Now you can use any stitch pattern you'd like to create the back of the sweater. I single crocheted in back loops only to make mine. I like making this sort of pattern because it makes the sweater stretchier. Crochet in each chain across.

3. Now continue to crochet in each stitch across until you have a rectangle piece measuring the length of your (C)Back Girth

measurement (as in the photo above). This is the top of your sweater that will cover your dog's back.

4. Now you're going to create the tummy portion. Begin to crochet in the next row as you have been, but don't go to the end - only go until you reach you (E) Tummy Length measurement. Stop here and turn your work.

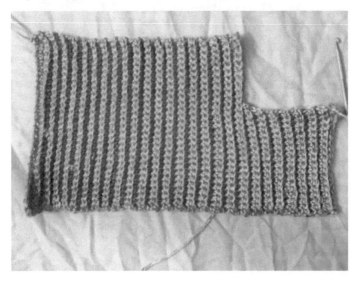

5. Chain 1, and continue your stitch pattern on these shorter rows until you make this small square your (D)Tummy Girth measurement. Now you have to body of your sweater.

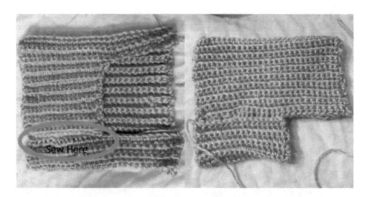

6. Now you'll sew the two ends together using your hook. Fold the tummy square over to the other side of the sweater so it looks like the picture above. Using your hook slip stitch the sides together. You can also choose to cast off first and sew the two sides together with a yarn hook, but I prefer this way since it's simpler and makes cleaner lines.

7. Now you'll be making your collar. Go to the front of your seater where the big opening is. Attach your yarn to the top of the rows (as shown) and crochet into the top of each row across. When you reach the end, chain enough stitch so that this whole side will measure the length of your (A) Collar measurement. Be sure to leave some extra lag here since you don't want it to be too tight if your dog ever gets stuck on something.

8. Once you have your length, attach your chain to the other side of the collar, where you attached your yarn. You now have a big circle the length of the collar measurement. Now you'll continue to crochet in rounds until the collar is as high as you'd like it to be. You can do one layer as I did, or you can make it longer and folded over.

And that's all there is to make this little sweater for your dog. As you can see, it's super easy to make for any size dog and can easily be adjusted with different stitch patterns to make it however you'd like. Of course, you could also add some cute buttons, embroidery, or mix up different colors of yarn.

Triple-Strand, Double-Belt Free Crochet Dog Sweater Pattern

Like the previous pattern, this one has a belt that wraps around the stomach. In fact, it has two! This makes for a unique design detail plus it secures the sweater comfortably around the pup as they move around. This crochet dog sweater is worked using three strands of yarn held together, so it's a bulky pattern that works up really quickly. It's practically a blanket. This pattern is designed for a dachshund but includes instructions for measuring to fit your own dog.

Measuring Dog

No two dogs are the same size. By measuring your dog you can make the sweater fit your canine buddy, no matter how big or small.

These instructions are for a standard sized dachshund.

Skill level: easy

3 skeins caron simply soft yarn

Crochet hook size k-10.5 (6.5 mm)

Gauge: 10 sc + 10 rows = approximately 4 in. (10 cm).

Back

Holding 3 yarn lengths together as one, ch 17.

Row 1. Sc in 2nd ch from hook and in each ch across – 16 sc.

Row 2. Ch 1 turn, 2 sc in first st, sc in each st across until reaching the last sc. 2 sc in last st.

Row 3-7. Repeat row 2. – 26 st.

Row 8. Ch 1 turn, 1 sc in each st across.

Repeat row 8 until sweater reaches 12". At this point you will increase for the neck band and begin to work in the round.

Neck band

After reaching the desired length of sweater finish the last row and then ch 15 st. Join last ch to first st of row and crochet in the round until neck band measures 1". Finish off by sl st in first sc.

Weave in ends.

Belly bands

First band:

Slip sweater over dog's head and mark where sweater edge is directly behind dog's front legs. Pick up 5 st. Right behind this mark.

Row 1. Ch 1, sc across – 5 st

Repeat row 1 until band measures 10". Make buttonhole.

Buttonhole row 1: ch 1, sc 2 st, ch 1, skip next sc, sc in last 2 st – 4 st

Buttonhole row 2: ch 1 sc 2 st, sc in c1, sc in last 2 st – 5 st

Repeat row 1 for 1" past buttonhole.

Finish off.

Weave in ends

Second band:

Pick up 5 st directly behind first band.

Repeat instructions for first band but shorten this band approximately 1" to allow for dog's "tummy tuck".

Finishing

Try the sweater on dog and mark for button placement. Sew buttons into place.

Simple Small Dog Crochet Sweater Pattern

This is an easy, free crochet dog sweater pattern designed specifically to fit Yorkies weighing about ten pounds. It is worked in basic crochet stitches, including single crochet and double crochet with just a little bit of back post crochet for fit and detail.

DIFFICULTY LEVEL: LEVEL 1 – BEGINNER

FINISHED DIMENSIONS:

Back measures about 9 1/2-inches from neck to end.

Chest measures about 6-inches from neck to belly.

GAUGE:

13 stitches and 4 rows = 4 – inches in double crochet

MATERIALS:

- Crochet Hook size J-6mm

- Percent Wool, Percent Acrylic

- Note: yarn is 4 Medium Worsted-weight, Afghan, Aran Yarn; 1-3/4-Ounce (50 g), 147 yd (135 m)

ABBREVIATIONS:

Stitch (St)

- Chain stitch (ch)

- Slip-stitch (slp st)

- Single crochet (sc)

- Double crochet (DC)

- Back post only (BPO)

- Single crochet 2 together (Sc2tog) – This is called making a decrease and it is actually very easy to do! So, please don't be put off by this. You can do it!

BACK:

~ Start at the neckline and work towards the tail.

Chain 31

Row 1: DC in 2nd ch from hook working in the BPO and then across (30 sts).

Rows 2: Ch 2, turn work, DC in 1st DC from hook and then across (30 sts)

Row 3: Repeat row 2.

~ Do not bind off. Fold collar in half lengthwise, SC through both halves across the bottom to seal the collar. when you reach the end, do not bind off, simply go ahead to row 4.

Row 4: Ch 2, turn work, DC across.

Rows 5 –18: Repeat row 4.

Row 19: Ch2, turn work, Sc2tog the first two stitches, Dc across, Sc2tog the last two stitches. (28 sts)

~ Each time you Sc2tog it reduces your stitch count by one. Since you did it twice in row 19, your stitch count should now be 28 sts.

Row 20: Repeat row 19. (26 sts)

Row 21: Ch 2, turn work, Dc in the next 12 stitches, Sc2tog the next two stitches, Dc in the last 12 stitches. (24 sts)

CHEST:

~ Start at belly end and crochet towards the neck.

Chain 18

Row 1: DC in the 2nd ch from hook and in each ch across. (17 sts)

Rows 2 – 5: Ch 2, turn work, DC across.

Rows 6 – 13: Ch2, turn work, Sc2tog the first two stitches, Dc across, Sc2tog the last two stitches.

~ Remember this reduces your stitch count by two for each row because you have Sc2tog twice.

Row 14: There should be only 2 stitches left. Sc2tog these last 2 stitches.

The chest piece should essentially be a triangle shape.

ASSEMBLY:

Place chest piece in the center of back pieces with right sides together. The tip of the chest piece should be at the base of the neck. So that when the chest piece is seamed in, there will a slight opening in the neck.

Use slip-stitch (slp st) to seam together the slight opening in the neck.

Use slip-stitch (slp st) to seam in the chest piece.

Leave about a 2-inch hole on each side for legs.

NOTE: Sweaters are machine washable, but do not exceed 400C water temperature.

Crochet Bumble Bee Sweater for Dogs

Dress your pooch up like a bumble bee with this cute crochet sweater. Most of the effect comes from the black-and-yellow stripes. However, don't forget those cute wings! Use this as a Halloween costume, for a photo shoot, or just to make your dog look adorable.

Skill Level:

Easy

Materials:

1. Yarn: #4 Medium Worsted Weight

Color A - Black

Color B - Bright Yellow

2. Crochet Hook – I/9 US - 5.5 MM - 5 UK

3. Yarn Needle (blunt sewing needle with big eye)

4. Measuring Tape (for measuring your dog)

Stitch Abbreviations:

sc – single crochet

sl st – slip stitch

ch – chain

Finished Size:

13 inches long

8 inches wide

Pattern is made for a long, medium sized dog

Important Note:

Resources for Measuring and Crocheting Sweaters for your Dog:

Everyone's dog is shaped differently, and it can be frustrating when most dog crochet patterns (like this one) are only written for a certain sized dog. Because of this potential obstacle, several of my readers have asked me how to alter my pattern so that it would fit their dog. So instead of giving them an estimated answer, I researched and found a free eBook that will not only teach you how to crochet a custom fit sweater for your dog, but will also provide the instruction you need to modify any crochet pattern for your dog by using a simple measure-to-fit-pattern concept.

Crochet Dog Sweater Pattern Instructions

Beginning at Collar

Foundation Chain: With color A (Black) ch 6.

Row 1: Sc in 2nd ch from hook and in remaining 4 ch's (5 sc).

Rows 2-42: Ch 1, sc in each sc across.

Fasten off by leaving an 8-12 inch tail for weaving.

Whip stitch both sides of collar together by using a yarn needle.

Weave in loose yarn ends.

Upper Body

Note: Weave in loose yarn ends while you work.

Rnd 1: Attach color B (Yellow) to any sc space on long edge of collar, sc in each sc around (42 sc).

Rnd 2: (Sc in next 2 sc, 2 sc in next sc) repeat around (56 sc).

Rnds 3-4: Sc in each sc around.

Rnd 5: Attach color A, sc in each sc around (56 sc).

Rnds 6-8: Sc in each sc around.

Sl st into next sc and fasten off.

Middle Back

Note: You will now be working in rows.

Row 9: Attach color B into sl st, ch 1, sc in next 37 sc (37 sc).

Rows 10-12: Ch 1, turn work, sc in each sc across .

Row 13: Attach color A, ch 1, turn work, sc in each sc across (37 sc).

Rows 14-16: Ch 1, turn work, sc in each sc across.

Row 17: Attach color B, ch 1, turn work, sc in each sc across (37 sc).

Rows 18-20: Ch 1, turn work, sc in each sc across.

Fasten off, weave loose yarn strand into sweater with a yarn needle.

Leg Holes and Stomach

Note: You will now be working on top of the 8th round and on the 9th row

Row 9: Skip 5 sc, attach color B into 6th sc and work a sc in same sp, sc in next 7 sc (8 sc).

Rows 10-12: Ch 1, turn work, sc in next 8 sc (8 sc).

Row 13: Attach color A, ch 1, turn work, sc in each sc across (8 sc).

Rows 14-16: Ch 1, turn work, sc in each sc across.

Row 17: Attach color B, ch 1, turn work, sc in each sc across (8 sc).

Rows 18-20: Ch 1, turn work, sc in each sc across.

Fasten off and weave in loose end.

Lower Torso

Note: You will now be working in rounds.

Rnd 21: Attach color A into the beginning stitch of the middle back, sc in each 37 sc around, ch 5, sc in next 8 sc, ch 5, sl st into the first sc that was made on rnd 21 (45 sc) (10 ch).

Rnd 22: Sc in each sc and in each ch sp around (55 sc).

Rnds 23-24: Sc in each sc around.

Rnd 25: Attach color B, sc in each sc around (55 sc).

Rnds 26-28: Sc in each sc around.

Rnd 29: Attach color A, sc in each sc around (55 sc).

Rnds 30-32: Sc in each sc around.

Rnd 33: Attach color B, sc in each sc around (55 sc).

Rnds 34-36: Sc in each sc around.

Hind End

Note: You will now be working in rows.

Row 37: Attach color A, sc in the next 37 sc (37 sc).

Rows 38-40: Ch 1, turn work, sc in each sc across.

Row 41: Attach color B, ch 1, turn work, sc in each sc across (37 sc).

Rows 42-44: Ch 1, turn work, sc in each sc across.

Row 45: Attach color A, ch 1, turn work, sc in each sc across (37 sc).

Rows 46-48: Ch 1, turn work, sc in each sc across.

Ruffle

Row 49: Ch 3, turn work (3 dc in next sc) repeat this pattern across row (111 dc).

Fasten off and weave in loose end.

This Sweater Also Looks Great in Different Colors!

Belted Crochet Dog Sweater Pattern for Chihuahua

The chihuahua gets cold really easily. Therefore, you might need a free crochet dog sweater pattern if you have one of these dogs. This adorable free pattern has a belt that wraps around the tummy, secured with two large, beautiful buttons. It's worked in single crochet and half double crochet, sometimes using the back loop only.

Materials Required:

4.5mm Crochet hook.

Row markers.

Darning needle.

Red Yarn. Medium 4.

2X 1 inch buttons.

1 Larger button (optional for collar).

Gauge:

Approximately 4 rows = 2 inches.

Approximately 6 hdc = 2 inches.

Special Abbreviations:

Ch = Chain.

Sc = Single Crochet.

Ea = Each.

St(s) = Stitch(es).

Mnr = Mark New Row/Round.

Rnd(s) = Round(s).

Beg = Beginning.

Ss = Slip Stich.

Hdc = Half Double Crochet.

Bl = Back Loop.

Instructions:

Starting with the collar.

Row 1: Ch 20. Turn. Hdc in 2nd ch from hook. Hdc in ea ch across. (19hdc)

Rows 2-18: Ch 2. Turn. Hdc in ea bl across, forming 'hills and valleys'. (19hdc)

Collar should measure approximately 5 1/2 inches X 10 inches.

Fold project in half, lining row 1 evenly up to row 18. Evenly ss through bl of both rows at same time, forming a tube (collar).

Working right to left, ss 6 times across to next 'hill'.

The Body:

Row 1: Ch 2. *Hdc in next st. Hdc in next valley, hdc in next st, hdc in next hill.* Repeat from * to * 6 more times. Hdc in next hill. (28hdc)

Row 2: Ch 2. Turn. Hdc in next 12 sts. Ch 4. Sk next 4 sts (Forming leash hole). Hdc in next 12 sts. (24hdc)

Rows 3-6: Ch 2. Turn. Hdc in ea st across. (28hdc)

Project should measure approximately 10 inches across.

Row 7: Ch 2. Turn. Hdc in ea st across. Ch 21. (28hdc, 21ch)

Row 8: Turn. Hdc in 2nd ch from hook. Hdc iin ea ch and st across. (47hdc)

Row 9: Ch 2. Turn. Hdc in next 44 sts. Ch 1. Sk next st (Forming button hole). Hdc in last 2 sts. (46hdc)

Row 10: Ch 2. Turn. Hdc in ea st across. Sk last st. (46hdc)

Row 11: Ch 2. Turn. Hdc in next 43 sts. Ch 1. Sk next st (Forming a button hole). Hdc in last 2 sts. (45hdc)

Row 12: Ch 2. Turn. Hdc in ea st across. Sk last st. (45hdc)

Strap should measure approximately 16 inch long with 2 button holes.

Row 13: Ch 2. Turn.Hdc in next 22 sts. (22hdc)

Rows 14-18: Ch 2. Turn. Hdc in ea st across. (22hdc)

Row 19: Turn. Hdc in ea st across. Sk last st.(21 hdc)

Row 20: Repeat Row 19. (19hdc)

Row 21: Repeat Row 19. (17hdc)

Row 22: Repeat Row 19. (15hdc)

Row 23: Repeat Row 19. (13hdc)

Row 24: Repeat Row 19. (11hdc)

Round 1: Ch 1 (mnr). Turn. Evenly sc around. Ss in beg ch 1 to join. (168sc) Fasten off. Weave in the ends.

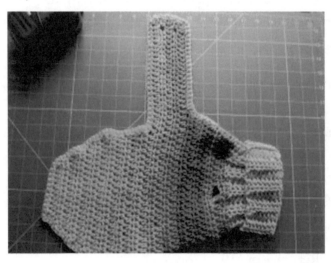

Try the sweater on your model. Line up the strap and sew buttons in place.

Made in United States
Troutdale, OR
11/13/2023

14543652R00033